BLOCKCHAIN

Understanding the Blockchain Revolution and the Technology Behind It

TABLE OF CONTENTS

INTRODUCTION

I want to thank you and congratulate you for purchasing the book, *"Blockchain: Understanding the Blockchain Revolution and the Technology Behind It"*.

This book contains proven steps and strategies on how to understand fully what a blockchain is, what the revolution is all about and the technology that is behind it all, driving one of the biggest innovations in IT for many years.

You will learn what a blockchain is, and then what the blockchain technology is. I will talk about how blockchain technology is going to change the world we live in irrevocably and forever.

Many of you have probably heard the term, "blockchain", many times over the last few years. That's because it is the technology that underpins the Bitcoin, the digital currency that more and more people are turning to. Banks believe that the blockchain could become the future of all financial transactions and governments are being strongly urged to adopt the technology as a permanent and tamper-free way of storing data and transactions.

Now I'm going to take you into the world of blockchain, the technology that drives it and what it means for us in the future.

Thanks again for purchasing this book, I hope you enjoy it!

PART 1

UNDERSTANDING THE BLOCKCHAIN AND
THE TECHNOLOGY BEHIND IT

CHAPTER 1

WHAT IS A BLOCKCHAIN?

A blockchain is a database that holds a series of records in a list that is ever expanding. Each record is called a block and the blockchain is fully secured from any form of tampering and from revision. Each of the records, or blocks, is time stamped and is also linked to the record before it, hence the chain.

We all know of blockchains as being the underlying technology of the virtual currency, the bitcoin. The idea of the bitcoin was born in 2008 and in 2009 it became a reality and the blockchain is actually a public ledger of every bitcoin transaction. In the case of the bitcoin, each client can connect to the network and can send transactions to the network. They can also verify transactions, and take part in the heavy competition to make new blocks, a competition known as mining.

A Brief History

When it was first thought of, the blockchain really was only for the bitcoin and was derived as the answer to making databases completely secure and with the ability to be distributed widely. From 2014, the term "blockchain 2.0" began to be used in the database field and this second-generation blockchain was described by The Economist as having a "programmable language that allows users to write more sophisticated smart contracts, thus creating invoices that pay themselves when a shipment arrives or shares certificates which automatically send their owners dividends if profits reach a certain level".

In 2016, a pilot project based on blockchain technology was announced by the central securities depository of the Russian Federations and a number of music industry regulatory bodies have begun to test out models for the collection of royalties and copyright management using blockchain technology.

How a Blockchain is Formed

Each blockchain is made up of blocks, each of which holds a valid transaction. Each of the blocks will include a hash of the block before it and this is what links the two together. These links form the chain. As well as containing a hash-based history, every blockchain database will also contain a specific algorithm. This is used to score different versions of the histories and this enables one version of a higher value to be chosen above the others. Peers that support the blockchain databases do not have access to the same versions of the history all of the time, instead, they just hang onto the version that scores the highest (at least that they know of). When a peer gets a newer version with a higher score, it will normally be the one they already have with a new block added to the chain. At this point, they will overwrite the database that they hold and then send the improvement to the other peers. However, there is absolutely no guarantee that one entry will stay in the highest scoring database version forever but, as a blockchain is built to add on the score of a new block to the total score of the existing blocks, there is a low probability of an entry being superseded, especially as more blocks go on and because there are certain incentives to working in adding new blocks to extend, rather than working just with old blocks.

Decentralization

By the very fact that a blockchain stores data across the network, it cuts out the risks that always go with centrally held data. This is because the network does not have the centralized points that are vulnerable, and this means hackers cannot exploit them. We all know that the internet has a ton of security problems today; how many of us still rely on the system of usernames and passwords to protect data and identity and these are easily hacked whereas the blockchain uses encryption technology for security.

Encryption technology is based on a system of private and public keys. The public key is a long string of numbers, generated randomly and this is the blockchain address of the user. The transaction that goes across the network is recorded on that key and is down as belonging to that specific user. The private key, on the other hand, is similar to a password and it is what allows the owner access to their digital assets. If you store data on a blockchain, it cannot be corrupted but you will need to take some extra measures – you need to create a paper wallet, and print your private key to safeguard it.

Every single node that is contained in a decentralized system contains a copy of the blockchain. There is no official centralized copy anywhere and no one user is given any more trust than another. All transactions are sent to the network through the use of the software. Mining nodes are then used to validate each of the transactions and then add them to the blockchain that is being created. The entire block is then sent to the other nodes. Each change is serialized through the use of timestamps.

In the beginning, blockchains used to be permission less and this has led to a certain amount of controversy over whether a permissioned database containing chained data blocks should actually be known as a blockchain. This is an ongoing debate and the crux of it is whether private systems that have verifiers who are tasked by and authorized by a central authority should actually be a blockchain.

Those in favor of private chains say that the term, "blockchain" should be applied to all data structures that put batches of time stamped data because the blockchains are a distributed version of MVCC (multi version concurrency). MVCC will not allow two transactions to concurrently make any modifications to an object within a database and, in the same way, blockchains also stop two transactions from spending a single output within a blockchain.

Opponents say that a permissioned blockchain looks very much like a traditional database and doesn't support decentralized data verification. These systems are not safe from tampering and are not secure from being revised by the operators. According to the Harvard Business Review, a blockchain is a "distributed ledger or database that is open to anyone" and Computerworld says that most of the hype that surrounds blockchains is nothing more than "snake oil and spin".

Applications

The blockchain technology, which I will talk about in more detail later on, can be integrated into several areas, including digital currency, payment systems, crowd sale facilitations, implementation of prediction markets and generic tools for governance. Major blockchain applications include:

Cryptocurrency:

- Bitcoin

- Ripple

- BlackCoin

- Nxt

- Dash

Blockchain Platforms:

- Factom – distributed registry

- MainSafe – software for decentralized applications

- Gems – decentralized messaging

- Stori – distributed cloud

- Tezos – decentralized voting

Applications

According to a research project carried out over 2 years by the Harvard business review, blockchain technology can be used to store and host, in a secure environment:

- Money

- Titles

- Deeds

- Music

- Art

- Intellectual property

- Scientific discoveries

- Votes

CHAPTER 2

UNDERSTANDING THE BLOCKCHAIN TECHNOLOGY

There is absolutely no doubt that the focus that was once on the single cryptocurrency (bitcoin) is fast moving towards applications that are based on cryptocurrency and built on the blockchain. The technology behind a blockchain is pretty much the same as that in a database but with one exception – the way that we interact with them is different.

For a developer, the concept of the blockchain is a radical change in the way that software applications of the future will be written. It is a key concept that has to be thoroughly understood, along with the other 4 of the 5 main concepts. We also need to understand how the concepts interrelate in the context of the blockchain technology. Those key concepts are:

1. The blockchain itself
2. The decentralized consensus
3. Trusted computing
4. Smart contracts
5. Proof of work

This paradigm is very important because it is the drive behind the creation of the decentralized application, the next step up in the evolution of the architectural constructs of distributed computing.

But this is by no means only a computing wonder. Applications that have been decentralized are going to be able to enable a trend of decentralization at 4 levels – business, governance, legal and societal. This is because the race is on to make everything decentralized and put the power at the edge of the networks. Let's take a look at each of these concepts in more detail:

1. The Blockchain and the Blockchain Services

A blockchain is a place where data is stored semi publicly in a block. Anyone can see who verified the block because it will have a signature on it but the only ones who can actually unlock the data inside the block are you or a specified program. This is because only the owner of the data has the private key to unlock it.

So, a blockchain is pretty much like a database with the exception that the header, or part of the stored information, is actually public. Stored data can be a balance of cryptocurrency or a toke of some value. In essence, the blockchain is an alternative system for value transfer, one that can be tampered with by malicious third parties or accessed by centralized agencies. The encryption is based on public and private keys – public visibility but only for private inspection. Your home address could be publicly advertised but it wouldn't give any information about how to get in your home or what it is like inside. That can only be done through a private key and, as that address has been claimed as yours, no one else can claim it.

The blockchain is also a software approach that binds several peer computers together, all of which will obey the consensus process of the release of information or for recording what information is held and is also where every interaction is cryptographically verified.

2. The Decentralized Consensus

This breaks the existing model of the centralized consensus, for example, when a central database was used to rule over the validity of transactions. Decentralized schemes, which the blockchain is based on, transfer the authority and the trust over to a virtual network that has been decentralized, thus allowing the nodes to record all transactions, on a continuous basis and in sequence, on public blocks, thus creating the chain. Each block contains a fingerprint, or a hash, of the block before it. Cryptography is used as a way of securing the authentication of each source though the use of these hashes and that eliminates the requirement or the need for any centralized intermediately. The combination of the blockchain technology and the cryptography ensures that no transaction is ever recorded in duplicate.

There is an important factor in this unbundling – the consensus logic is kept separated from the application, which means that the application can be specifically written to be decentralized. That is the dynamite that is needed to kick off a whole series of system-changing innovations within the application software architecture, whether they are related to money or not.

3. Trusted Computing

Or, as some call it, trustless transactions. When you put together the concepts that are behind the blockchain – the smart contracts and the decentralized consensus – you begin to see that they are actually helping transactions and resources to spread in a lateral peer-to-peer manner and, in doing so, they are also enabling the computer to have trust in one another at a very deep level.

Where central organizations and institutions are seen as necessary to be trusted authorities, some of the centralized functions can actually be codified in a smart contract that is under the governance of a decentralized consensus on the blockchain.

Because the blockchain has the role of validating transactions, each of the peers can go head and trust each other because living on the technology are a number of rules:

- Trust

- Compliance

- Governance

- Authority

- Contracts

- Law

- Agreements

If you look ahead to the future, not too far ahead, smart property and smart contracts will be automatically created and executed between parties without either knowing that the blockchain was even involved as the trusted intermediary.

4. Smart Contracts

These are building blocks for the decentralized application. Smart contracts are like small programs that you can give a unit of value to, whether it is money or a token, along with the rules that govern that value. The idea behind the smart contract is so that any contractual governance between at least two parties for each transaction can be verified via the blockchain. There is no need to have a centralized agency when the parties can come to an agreement between them and when they can put the terms and the implications of the agreement directly into the program. Those terms include the fulfillment of services sequentially and penalties if a transaction is not fulfilled.

When you apply a smart contract, you assume that there is no need for a third-party intermediary to conduct any transaction between two or more parties. Instead, the parties will come to an agreement between them on the definition of the rules and ensure that they are embedded within the transaction. This means that the end-to-end resolution is self-managed between the computers that are representing the user interest. A smart property is a digital asset that knows exactly who its owner is and the ownership is generally linked into the blockchain.

5. Proof of Work

At the very heart of the operations in a blockchain is this concept. Proof of work was an important part of the original blockchain role as the transaction authenticator. Proof of work is what provides the right to take part in the blockchain and it is displayed as a large hurdle that stops users from making changes to records stored on the chain without providing a new proof of work.

It is one of the main building blocks simply because it can never be undone and is cryptographically secured through the hashes that are used to prove its authenticity. However, it an expensive concept to maintain, estimated to cost about $600 million a year jut for bitcoin and that means there could be future issues of scalability and security. This is because it depends entirely on the incentives for the miners – mining will decline as time goes by. A better solution is called "proof of stake" – much cheaper for enforcing but way more expensive and much more difficult to compromise. This concept will determine who is allowed to update the consensus and stop the underlying blockchain from being forked.

Moving Towards Decentralization

In the near future, we will be facing a rush to come up with decentralized applications that enable the new decentralized world we are fast heading for. Because of that, both visionaries and business leaders will have to learn a brand new vocabulary that based on crypto frameworks. Developers are going to have to learn how to write these decentralized apps that will be enabled by the technology behind the blockchain. And the end-user has to learn all about the smart contract, how to create them and how to use them. Developmental environments will need to be comprehensive and will need to support a whole range of capabilities and components on the blockchain services and on the consensus engine.

Blockchain technology for the bitcoin had a number of limitations that came to light as we began to push it outside of services that were related to money and into the realms of software applications. We really shouldn't be surprised that multiple blockchains as the way forward and some of them will work together, others will compete against one another while yet others will simply be benevolent.

These decentralized apps will be all different sizes, different flavors and the whole range of complexity levels so we have to be fully prepared for all of the variety. We have to be able to see beyond what the bitcoin promised and right into the heart of the blockchain promise to become the brand new environment development, in the same way that, back in 1996, web development was the environment.

That said, decentralized applications cannot be used for everything and we will find that some things simply won't fit into the paradigm of the decentralized application. There are a number of applications that do fit the bill and that gives us a nice number of opportunities or visionaries, creators, and developers to take advantage of. We will call them blockchain apps for now.

Emerging Blockchain Application Segments

There are four of these and I will discuss each one in turn:

- Currency

- Pegged Services

- Smart Contracts

- Distributed Autonomous Organization

Currency

This segment is aimed at payments, monetary transfers, tips, and funding applications. The end users will either use an exchange or their own wallet for these types of transactions and they reap the benefits of reductions in the transaction costs, a speedy settlement and not having to go through a centralized agency. Today, exchanges have been centralized but we are likely to see a future generation of trusted exchanges that are decentralized. Although the wallets used for bitcoin are classed as "dumb", future wallets are likely to become smarter with the ability to launch a smart contract.

Pegged Services

This is a rather interesting segment. Services that are pegged to the blockchain are able to make use of the atomic unit in the chain. This is a capability that stores values but the pegged service can also build on that with their own off-chain services. An example of this would be a decentralized ownership or agency, which is horizontal service, being able to be applied to any vertical segment, such as photography, music, or videos, to name just a few.

Smart Contracts

We already know what the smart contract is but, in terms of the segment, they are representative of a simple decentralization form. They are expected to become fully available in several application areas, for example, family trusts, wagers, time stamping, escrow, proof of work, etc. In short, they are all about the movement of value or assets between owners, based on a condition or an event. They are representative of an "intermediate state" between two or more parties and we will place trust in them to verify and to take logic-based action behind the changes in the state.

Distributed Autonomous Organization

Putting aside legal issues, these are sort incorporated on the blockchain. This is because the governance of them is dependent on the end-user. The end-user is a part-users, a part owner, and part-node on the decentralized network. The key parts of a DAO are that every user is a worker and by virtue of that, they make some contribution to the appreciation of the value of the DAO through their activity or participation.

Examples of the Segment Uses

- **Currency Category** – Protocol users are payment processors, wallets, miners, and exchanges. Their frequency is sporadic and the benefits are speed and cost

- **Pegged Services Category** – Protocol users are web businesses and their frequency is chronic. Benefits are flexibility, empowered users, openness, network effects and new business models

- **Smart Contracts Category** – Protocol users are web apps, contract service providers, end-users with the use of self-service tools and their frequency is episodic. Benefits are cost, autonomy, speed and irrefutability

- **Decentralized Autonomous Organizations Category** – Protocol users are the DAO itself and the frequency is habitual. Benefits include user voice, user protection, user governance, sovereignty, self-regulation, and transparency.

There are probably more categories but these are the most important ones and the examples are purely a sample. However, for each and every segment, users should be asking themselves two questions – "what is the benefit?" and "Is there a good reason why I should participate?" The provider of the blockchain applications should focus their attention on answering these two questions in the clearest and most compelling way possible. The end-user is the fuel that fires the engine of the application success and it is, therefore, vital to stay near to the potential of the network effects on blockchain applications

PART 2

POTENTIAL USES FOR THE BLOCKCHAIN TECHNOLOGY

CHAPTER 3

THE BANKING INDUSTRY

There are a number of different potential uses for the blockchain technology, including, with use cases:

- **Technology Decentralization**

Financial institutions and banks have been very active in investing both money and time into this area. We will now take a look at some of these institutions who are showing true interest in the blockchain:

- **Deutsche Bank**

The Deutsche bank has been investing heavily into looking at the use cases of the blockchain in the regions of fiat currency settlement, payments, enforcement, asset registries, clearing derivative contracts, KYC, improving the processing services post-trade, regulatory reporting, etc. It has run several experiments on the technology in the innovation labs in Silicon Valley, Berlin, and London

- **NASDAQ**

The NASDAQ stock exchange revealed recently that they were going to be using blockchain as a business-wide technology to improve their qualification on the Private Market Platform. This is a brand new initiative that started in 2014 and enables Pre-IPO trading between private companies. The stock exchange has also revealed that they will use the clout of the Open Assets Protocol to build up their own private platform. Later on, they then announced that they had gone into a partnership with a blockchain infrastructure called Chain, a provider specifically aimed at financial institutions and business users.

- **DBS Bank**

DBS bank was responsible for organizing and initiating a Blockchain hackathon. They did this in conjunction with Coin Republic, a bitcoin company based in Singapore. The APIs for the hackathon, which lasted for two days were provided by Blockstrap, BitX and Colu and the winners were an investment platform aimed at the emerging markets, called Omnichain. Nubank, a provider of "banking for the unbanked" came in second and BlockIntel, a transactions security platform came third.

- **EBA**

The Euro Banking Association released a report in 2015 that discussed the impact of using crypto-technology from the perspective of payment professional and transaction banking in the next three years. The report noted that the technology could be used with authority by banks to cut down their audit and governance costs, to provide a better time-to-market and much better products

- **US Federal Reserve**

The USFR is reported to be working together with IBM on the development of a new digital blockchain-based payment system

- **SCB**

According to a posting made on LinkedIn, the chief innovation officer of the Standard Chartered Bank, Anju Patwardhan, says that blockchains could be used to cut down on costs and on improving the transparency of all financial transactions.

As well as these, there are also reports that CME Group, and Deutsche Boerse, both derivatives companies, along with clearing houses EuroCPP and DTCC are all working on projects that surround using blockchain in clearing, amongst other areas. And, there has been talk of Western Union possible looking into the use of Ripple technology

Below are some of the banks that are experimenting with the use of Blockchain:

- **Fidor Bank**

The bank has entered a partnership with Bitcoi.de, a German peer-to-peer BTC trading Platform and with Kraken to come up with an exchange for digital currency within the EU. They also partnered up with Ripple Labs so that they could provide money transfer services

- **LHV Bank**

This bank is reported to have begun working on the blockchain technology back in 2014 and, since then, have come up with an app called Cuber Wallet, based on colored coins. They have also gone into partnership with Coinfloor and Coin base to experiment with blockchain-based digital security

- **CBW Bank and Cross River Bank**

Both have gone into partnership with Ripple Labs to come up with a risk management system and to provide remittance services at a lower cost.

- **Rabobank, ING Bank, and ABN Amro**

All are currently exploring the blockchain technology for a number of different services Rabobank has also gone into partnership with Ripple Labs

- **Goldman Sachs**

Goldman Sachs were the lead investors in Circle Internet Financial Ltd, a bitcoin startup that required initial funding of $50 million.

- **BBVA Ventures**

BBVA are Coinbase investors and have also released a report stating that they are fully interested in the use of blockchain technology

- **Santander**

Santander claims that they have at least 20-25 use cases for the blockchain technology and has set up a dedicated team called Crypto 2.0 to investigate how blockchains can be used in banking

- **Westpac**

Westpac has gone into partnership with Ripple Labs to come up with a low-cost system of cross-border payments. Its venture capital arm, called Reinventure, took part in the Series C funding venture for Coinbase.

- ## UBS

UBS has a cryptocurrency lab based in London and is currently running experiments on trading and settlement, payments and smart bonds. It has a plan to build a product called the "utility settlement coin" in a partnership with Clearmatic and they also claim to have between 20 and 25 uses in the financial sector for the blockchain

- ## BNY Mellon

BNY have come up with BK Coins, their own currency, and use it as a recognition program in the corporation. The coins can be redeemed for gifts or rewards.

- ## Barclays Bank

Barclays bank has 2 bitcoin labs, based in London, that are used by a number of different blockchain entrepreneurs, businesses, and coders. They have also entered into a partnership with Safello and are currently working on developing different banking services based on the blockchain. They run accelerators to give blockchain enthusiasts a bit of mentoring and give them the chance to work on specific projects with the bank and they claim to have around 45 different blockchain-based projects that they want to work on internally

- ## CBA

Has gone into partnership with Ripple Labs to come up with a blockchain-based ledger system for use in payment settlements between its own subsidiaries

- **USAA Bank**

Have created their own research team to implement a study of the bitcoin uses

- **ANZ Bank**

Have entered into a partnership with Ripple Labs to look at the uses of blockchain

- **BNP Paribas**

Are currently running experiments on how to use blockchain to make transactions faster

- **Societe Generale**

Are planning on employing staff that have expertise in blockchain, BTC, and cryptocurrency

- **Citibank**

Citibank has set up three systems that are used to deploy blockchain technology and have also developed their own form of the bitcoin, called Citicoin. This is currently being used within Citibank as a way of learning how the digital currency trading system works

CHAPTER 4

Examples Of Public And Private Blockchain Concepts

The Public Blockchain

Public blockchains are platforms where anyone who is on the platform can read it or write to it. They must be able to provide proof of work, though. This area has seen quite a lot of growth in activity, as the number of potential users that blockchain technology can generate is very high. On top of that, the public blockchain is considered a decentralized blockchain. Some examples of this include:

- **Ethereum** – providers of a programming language and a decentralized platform that is for helping startup contracts and also lets developers publish their distributed applications

- **Factom** – providers of records business processes and records management for governments and other businesses

- **Blockstream** – providers of a sidechain technology that is focused on extending the capabilities that bitcoin currently has. They have now begun experiments on using public blockchain technology for providing accounting, a function that was once considered to be done on the private blockchain.

Private Blockchains

Private blockchains are those that will only let the owner have the right to make changes that need to be made. This is somewhat similar to the infrastructure that already exists whereby the owner, which would be a centralized agency or authority, would have the power to revert transactions, change the rules, etc., based entirely on need. This concept is huge and could attract massive interest from financial institutions and large businesses and could, in theory, find use cases to come up with proprietary systems and cut costs while concurrently increasing efficiency. Some examples are:

- **Eris Industries** – they aim to be the only provider of shared software databases that make use of blockchain technology

- **Blockstack -** they aim to be the providers to the back office operations of financial institutions, including settlement and clearing on private blockchains

- **Multichain** – providers of a distributed database that is open source for financial transactions

- **Chain Inc.** – providers of APIs. They are chain partnered with the NAZDAQ OMX Group Inc. and provide platforms that allow the trading of private business shares using the blockchain

Hybrid Blockchain Concepts

Is there such a thing? A consortium blockchain would be a combination of a public and a private blockchain. This would mean that the ability to both read and write to it would be extended to several modes or people. This would be able to be used by companies who join forces and collaborate on the development of different models. As such, they could actually gain a blockchain that has restricted access, they could work together on their solutions and still maintain intellectual property rights inside of the consortium.

CHAPTER 5

FINANCIAL SERVICES – THE BLOCKCHAIN INNOVATION

Not since the internet first came into existence have we seen such an awesome innovation as the blockchain. The technology behind the blockchain allows every person to hold transactions and to make them as strangers but in a way that is totally transparent. There is no intermediary between the person making and the person receiving the transaction and the whole process is so much cheaper and easier. We can apply the blockchain concept to the whole digital world that is involved in making any kind of transaction or exchange secure, and this doesn't just apply to the bitcoin. There is a wide range of companies and business models that are starting to appear, based entirely on the blockchain technology and these next couple of chapters will take you through a number of them.

As you already know, a blockchain network is made up of distributed servers, or nodes. Each node shares the information about the transaction. As much as it all may sound very confusing, in actual fact, it is so much easier to understand the impressive business models that are based on the technology.

So far you have seen that the distributed ledger is a record of transactions that cannot be erased. The entire computer network, across the globe, that runs blockchain software takes care of the maintenance and the performance of the whole blockchain network. On average, around 6 times every hour, a new batch of transactions that have been accepted is created and this I called a block. It is added to the chain and published across all of the nodes, allowing the blockchain software to decide when a specific transaction has taken place.

It is this very feature of the technology that has expanded in popularity amongst the developers, the large banks, and the entrepreneurs. Along with Santander, who are already investigating the use of distributed ledgers and blockchain technology in the bank, both JP Morgan and Citibank have also shown a great deal of interest in using the technology.

A lot of startup businesses are also building up their business around the technology and, as a result, venture capital firms like KPCB are beginning to become interested in investing in them. Startups like Coinmetric gather research and data on the quantitative and qualitative behavior of blockchains, while other companies, like BTCJam, provide loans that are bitcoin-based. Yet others that are built on the technology include BitPay, BlockCypher, and BitPagos. One of the more interesting of these startups is called, simply, Chain and it helps other businesses to build up financial products that are based on blockchain technology, using its own Bitcoin API. NASDAQ has picked this company to help run a pilot on NASDAQ Private Market using the blockchain technology.

Some Use Cases and Initiatives

It is very evident that financial institutions are keenly interested in blockchain technology. Santander, as we mentioned earlier, have already come up with 20 to 25 different uses and have also estimated that banks who use blockchain technology can cut their infrastructure costs by up to an impressive $20 billion every year. UBS and Goldman Sachs have also set up labs to research blockchain technology and its uses within their own banks.

Right now, although you may think that the financial industry is the main focus here, in actual fact, it is non-financial uses that are taking the limelight. Over 50 different startups have appeared in the non-financial use category and Blockchain Capital, who used to be known as Crypto Currency Partners, has already raised more than $7 million towards an investment fund, their second in fact, for ventures that are related to both bitcoin and blockchain technology that relate only to non-financial uses.

Right now, the startups currently in this sector are focused mainly on the Internet of Things, asset servicing, documentary trade and identity management and it will be interesting to see how governments adopt the use cases to streamline their processes and those of the public sector.

31

CHAPTER 6

BLOCKCHAIN USES – FINANCIAL AND NON-FINANCIAL

The use cases of the blockchain technology have been growing as each day passes. As such, there has been a large variety of ways to which we could link real-world assets toe the blockchain and trade them digitally. Proof of concept is already being run for some of the bigger trading commodities, like bars of gold, diamond, and silver, after they have been authenticated through the blockchain. Following those, we also have the provision of voting, the establishment of real estate ownership, etc.

Quite apart from the startup businesses, financial institutions like the banks have been investing in the decentralized system and many are actively experimenting and researching how the blockchain technology can be used. Below, we look at the broad applications that some companies are providing through blockchain technology, financial and non-financial:

- **Development of apps** – proof of module ownership within app development

- **Digital Content** – Proof of ownership for the delivery and storage of digital content

- **Ride-Sharing** – a value transfer based on points for ride-sharing

- **Digital Security Trading** – Ownership/transfer

- **Digitization of Contracts and Documents** – including proof of ownership in the case of transfers

- **Decentralized Storage** – using a computer network that is on the blockchain

- **Company Incorporations** – the digitization of incorporations and the transfer of ownership and equity

- **Decentralization of Internet and Computing Resources** – Including those that cover all homes and businesses

- **Home Automation** – a platform that links the home network and connected devices to the cloud

- **Digital Identity** – Provision of digital identities that are sued to protect consumer privacy

- **Escrow and Custodian Services** – specific to the gaming industry, e-commerce and load servicing

- **IT Portal** – Smart contract that executes the fulfillment of orders in manufacturing and e-commerce

- **Patient Records** – the decentralization of patient record management services

- **Digitization of Assets** – Helps to improve measures for anti-counterfeiting

- **Reputation Management** – to help users to engage and share reputation, collecting feedback as well

- **Prediction Platform** – a decentralized platform for share market prediction

- **Enabling Review Authenticity** – using endorsements that are trustworthy for employee peer reviews

- **Sale and Purchase of Digital Assets** – a marketplace for the sale and purchase of digital assets and proof of ownership

CHAPTER 7

THE ROLE OF BLOCKCHAIN TECHNOLOGY IN FUTURE CAPITAL MARKETS

Blockchain technology has caused a real stir, particularly in the financial world. Many banks, venture capitalists, and other financial institutions are already looking into how blockchain technology can be used to store data and for other financial uses. One such financial industry is capital markets and it is here that the industry experts are showing the most enthusiasm and optimism about using blockchain technology to solve a number of issues.

Asset Movement

In order for assets to be moved from one financial institution to another, the ledger balances for the assets must also move. This is not an easy job and involves the use of several intermediaries. The more there are involved in the transaction, the more messages need to be exchanged and this results in even more updating of the ledgers required. In an average trade, there are already several intermediaries, including CCPs (central counterparties), exchanges, CSDs (central securities depositories, custodians, brokers and investment managers. In order for the accounting to be correct and for the transaction to be successfully completed, all of the intermediaries involved have to make sure their ledgers are updated based on the messages that are exchanged.

In essence, this means that whenever a transaction takes place, even more messaging needs to be carried out and this causes delays and adds to the total cost. On occasion, in order for a transaction to be completed and all the correct ledger updates made, the intermediaries may have to complete even more ledgers, such as securities borrowing, realignments or cash management. All this does is delay the transaction and is usually referred to, in capital market speak, as a settlement cycle.

So how can blockchain technology help? The creation of a shared flat ledger to process the transactions that happen between several intermediaries is the most important expectation of the capital market industry and will help in cutting both the time and the costs involved in each transaction. Using blockchain technology will also ensure that real-time asset transfers can easily be facilitated.

Financial industries can make use of blockchain technology to build shared flat ledgers that can easily be managed by processing nodes that are trusted. Through the use of digital signatures, the intermediaries will be able to update the ledgers to finish the business transaction. Shared ledgers have to be encrypted so that data confidentiality is maintained. The key processes that are involved in the execution of a trade, like trading, security clearance, settlement and clearing can easily be redesigned and made much simpler with the use of the blockchain.

Onboarding and Maintenance

Account maintenance and client onboarding is the next part of the capital market industry where blockchain technology is highly likely to be put to good use. KYC, or Know Your Customer, costs are incredibly high and cutting down on the cost and cutting out some of the KYC checks that need to be done is just what business the world over are looking to do. If they had a system built in the blockchain that both stored and facilitated Know Your Customer data, they can cut their costs and they can cut down on the amount of YC checks that need to be done. There are already a number of blockchain startup businesses that are focused on the improvement of identity management and we expect to see this number rise significantly over the coming years.

What About Payments?

Payments are a segment of the market where we can expect to see a substantial rise in the use of blockchain technology over the next few years. The blockchain technology can be used to customize the business rules for the processing of transactions, as well as help to tailor these rules to the specific business. This will all be based on the needs of the specific organization and the technology used would be open source software, enabling any number of businesses to use and tailor the software to their own requirements.

Areas that will see the biggest benefits of blockchain technology are bonds trading and OTC (over the counter) derivatives. The technology will be able to provide the business with a secure settlement model that is in real-time and is also cost effective to run, along with being decentralized and global. In short, it really is just a matter of time before the blockchain steps in and starts playing an immense role in capital markets.

A financial services company, based in Belgium and called Euroclear explains how blockchain technology can help the capital market sector. They say that, put basically, the records for every security would be placed onto a flat accounting basis, which means there would be "multiple levels of beneficial ownership" contained on each ledger. There would no more need to operating data normalization for reconciling internal systems or for agreements on exposure and obligation. There would be processes and services that are standardized, reference data would be shared, processing capabilities, like reconciliations, would be standardized, data would be near real-time and there would be a better understanding of the worthiness of counterparts. For regulators and other privileged participants, there would be better transparency on holdings data, along with a whole host of other improvements.

The Benefits for the Capital Market

According to Euroclear, the capital market segment would reap the following benefits:

Pre-Trade

- Better transparency of holdings

- Better verification of holding

- A reduction in credit exposures

- Mutualization of all static data

- Much easier KYC

Trade

- More secure transaction matching in real-time

- Immediate and irrevocable settlement of transactions

- Automatic cash ledger DVP

- Automatic reporting

- Better, more transparent supervision for the market authorities

- Higher standards in AML2

Post-Trade

- Real-time cash transactions do not need to go through central clearing

- Reduced margin requirements

- Reduced collateral requirements

- Interchangeable use of assets as collateral on the blockchain

- Automatic execution of all smart contracts

Securities Servicing and Custody

- Primary proceedings directly to the blockchain

- Automation of servicing processes

- De-duplication of servicing processes

- Better central datasets that have flat accounting orders

- Common data for reference

- Automatic processing of fund subscriptions and redemption directly on the blockchain

- More simplified method of fund servicing

- More simplified method of accounting

- Simpler methods of administration and allocation

Who are the Early Believers and the Pioneers of the Blockchain Technology?

On the Public Platform

1. **NASDAQ -** In December of 2015, NASDAQ released an official statement to say that Linq, its own blockchain ledger technology, had been successful in completing and recording a private securities transaction. This was the very first time this had been achieved using blockchain. NASDAQ Linq is a digital ledger that uses the blockchain to aid in the cataloging, issuance and recording of shares that are held in the Private Market by privately held companies. It is designed to complement the cloud-based capitalization management that NASDAQ Private Market, called ExactEquity. Linq clients will

be given a full historical and comprehensive record of the issue and transfer of their own securities, providing much better auditability, governance of issue and transfer of ownership.

2. **ASX** – the ASX is the largest stock exchange in Australia and it has now confirmed that it is working on the development of a private blockchain in conjunction with Digital Asset, a US-based firm, as a solution for post-trade in the Equity market in Australia. The ASX paid a sum of AUD $14.9 million to gain an equity interest of 5% in Digital Assets Holdings and this fee will be used to fund the first phase of the distributed ledger solution.

On the Private Platform

1. **Chain.com** – Chain is a blockchain startup that documents the use of the NASDAQ technology to issue shares to a private investor. The issuer of the securities used NASDAQ Linq to represent, in the digital sense, a record of ownership. The settlement time was reduced significantly and the paper stock certificates were, in effect, redundant. Linq also allows investors and issuers to complete subscription documents and then execute them, all online.

2. **Funderbeam** – this company is set to launch the very first investment trading platform that is based on the blockchain technology in the next few months. They will be doing this through a partnership with ChromaWay, a developer of colored coins. Each of the syndicates will be paired up with a micro fund and that micro fund will own real stakes in real startups. As such, when a member of the syndicate wants to trade some or all of their own holdings,

they will actually be trading digital stakes in the micro fund. The blockchain will be used to verify every transaction before it is enforced and the same thing happens when an investor decides to sell all or part of their digital stakes. In each of the investments, the change of ownership will have a distributed audit trail that is fully secure.

The Challenges Faced by the Capital Market in Adopting Blockchain Technology

The capital market will face a number of challenges that they will need to overcome if blockchain technology is to be adopted successfully:

1. **There must be very high standards set for the technology to succeed.** This is mainly for the security, for the performance and the robustness of the blockchains. Also, non-blockchain systems, like risk management platforms, will also have to be integrated at some point in the near future.

2. **Legislation and Regulations Must Be Upgraded.** In order for blockchain technologies to be successfully made an integral part of the infrastructure, new regulatory principles will need to be fully integrated.

3. **New Standards and Governance Will Be Required.** On some design points, industry alignment will be a requirement. Some of those points include whether the systems in use are fully open, like the bitcoin system, or whether they use a system of permission-based access; the principles that govern whether the system is

suitable for interaction with the ledger; whether different systems are interoperable – systems may be running difference safeguards against errors in coding or consensus protocols and this could create knock-on effects that may not be detectable to start with

4. **The Proper Management of the Transition to Minimize Operational Risk.** Operational risk is a big consideration and it must be minimized as far as possible.

Blockchain Companies Already Applying Distributed Ledger Security

These companies have already built their systems and are applying the blockchain-based distributed ledger technology to security and compliance

1. **Third-Key Solutions** – They provide cryptographic key management solutions and consulting to companies who use distributed blockchains, decentralized digital currencies and asset tokens

2. **Chainalysis** – provides products that let financial institutions spot the connections between two or more digital identities and develop lines of trust between them. The products can also help them to identify any malicious actors in the process. Chainalysis states that their mission is to come up with tools that stop any abuse of the system they are being applied to and that respect the privacy of users.

3. **Tradle** – uses the blockchain to bridge external and internal financial networks to achieve portability in KYC that is controlled

by the user. An open-source mobile framework has been combined with business app development and a full integration platform that allows Tradle to develop sophisticated full-stack blockchain apps

4. **Vogogo** – This company specializes in providing verification tools for both payment processing and for risk management. To do this they use a simple JSON REST API.

5. **Elliptic** – the first company in the world to secure blockchain asset insurance and to achieve accreditation from one of the Big Four Audit firms, KPMG. They offer AML bitcoin protection in real-time

6. **Civic** – an identity solution that is based on the blockchain, aiming to tackle consumer identity theft and to bring about a reduction in online identity fraud.

7. **Coinalytics** – this company allows enterprises to determine real-time risk assessment and intelligence from the decentralized applications and from blockchains. They use methodologies that are based on pattern recognition and on real-time learning online to mine simulated data with few features.

8. **Sig3** – The company uses multi-sig technology to provide extra security layers for transactions made through bitcoin Instead of a requirement for just one signature or one key to make a transaction, the user is able to set up a multi-sig wallet requiring the signature from two of three provided keys before the transaction can be completed and broadcast to the blockchain network. Because Sig3 is an independent automated third-party co-signer, it can be integrated into any multi-sig wallet while maintaining distance from said wallet. This ensures there is no point of failure.

9. **Blockseer** - This company has a mission to build a "unified foundation of transparency" for the public ecosystem for bitcoin. By providing the transparency of the blockchain and all of its participants, the company is aiming to cut down on the disorder and chaos and increase knowledge levels and analysis of the public blockchain network

10. **CryptoCorp** – This company is a security startup that is focused entirely on bringing about improvements to the bitcoin ecosystem. They offer a service that is called Digital Oracle, which can take part in multi-signature transactions that originate from any bitcoin wallet

11. **Blockverify** – A company that offers an anti-counterfeit system that is based on the blockchain. The system can be applied to luxury items, pharmaceuticals, diamonds and electronics and, using Blockverify, companies will be able to create their own product registers and monitor their own supply chains.

CHAPTER 8

BLOCKCHAIN APPLICATIONS BEYOND THE FSI

Blockchain fever is no way limited to the financial services industry, not by a long shot. As well as the banks and the financial tech startup companies, quite a few non-financial companies and industries have been paying quite a lot of attention to what is going on and are now looking for ways to make use of the opportunities that are offered by distributed ledger technology. In this chapter, we take a look at some of the most interesting examples of non-financial applications for blockchain technology.

Blockchain Technology and Commodities

The Real Asset Company allows people from all over the world to purchase silver and gold bullion in a secure and efficient way. They have an investor-friendly platform that is situated over the global vaulting infrastructure and which provides users with an online account for the purchase of silver and gold and for holding precious metal. Goldbloc is the gold-backed cryptocurrency used by the company that adds an extra layer of transparency and more control to the user's investment of gold. The company is backed up by a gram of gold and they fully believe that their cryptocurrency is the first step in bringing gold firmly back into the monetary system.

Uphold is another platform that is designed around the movement, conversion, transactions and holding of all forms of commodities or money. The business connects debit cards, credit cards, banks, and bitcoin to digital wallets for free transactions and financial services. Both consumers and businesses will be able to fund their accounts or by linking their credit or debit card or through bank transfer as well as bitcoin

Blockchain Technology and Diamonds

The diamond industry is probably the largest of all the natural resource industries and is a significant portion of the GDP in Africa and in other large diamond miners. The industry has one main hallmark – the fact that it is one of the most highly criminalized in the world. The stones are small and can easily be hidden and transported and the best bit about it for the criminal is that the transactions can take place in confidence and the sale will always return value over the years. Diamonds are well known to be firmly involved in the financing of terrorist activities and in money laundering on a massive scale the world over.

Because of the scale of the challenges with the diamond business, one of the technical pioneers, Everledger, is a company that provides an immovable ledger of the transaction verifications and identification for a number of stakeholders, from insurance companies right up to law enforcement agencies. Everledger assigns each diamond with its own digital passport that will accompany the stone through its transaction and also creates a unique fingerprint.

Blockchain Technology and Data Management

Factom is a leading and notable company in applying blockchain-based distributed ledgers to the non-financial sector, in particular, data management. Factom uses identity ledgers that are based on blockchain technology for data analytics and database management to support a number of different applications. Both governments and businesses can use Factom to make records management much simpler, along with easier record business processes. It can also be used to address issues surrounding security and compliance. Factom keeps a permanent record of all data in the blockchain, records that are timestamped, allowing companies to cut the complexity and the cost of auditing, records management and in complicity with government regulations.

Blockchain Technology and Cannabis

Serica is one of the blockchain companies that exists within the cannabis industry. They are responsible for bringing cryptofinance, software engineering, blockchain technology and financial custody to the traditional custodian finance model. The technology allows entrepreneurs to get their business set up legitimately, using the largest network of customers to grow their memberships, conversions, registrations and average order sizes. They use Secure Socket Layering (SSL) technology to encrypt all of the communication that takes place between Serica and the user's wallet. The blockchain is used to track every medical marijuana purchase and record them, giving the businesses the easy way to take online payments. Other

48

companies that used blockchain technology in the cannabis business are Tokken and Hypur.

Blockchain Technology and Digital Content

Ascribe is a company set up to help creators and artists to attribute their digital art through the blockchain. Their marketplace lets digital editions be generated with unique IDs and digital certificates of authenticity as a way of proving authenticity and provenance. It also lets consignments from artists be accepted and digital works transferred to collectors with all the relevant terms and legal conditions. Other companies that do the same kind of thing include Stampery, Blockai and Bitproof.

Blockchain Technology and the Network Infrastructure

Ethereum is both a programming language and a platform that allows any developer to build next-generation distributed applications and publish them. The company can be used to decentralize, codify, trade and secure just about anything you can think of, including voting, financial exchanges, domain names, company governance, crowd funding, agreements and contracts, smart property and intellectual property, all thanks to the hardware integration.

Another company who offers up blockchain technology as a platform for the financial industry is ChromaWay. They are also working on building a smart contract platform that will allow workflows to be digitized and represented in a private, secure and efficient way.

Blockchain Technology and Market Forecasting

Augur.net is a decentralized and open-source platform for market predictions that is built on the Ethereum blockchain it lets users trade on event outcomes and then uses the crowd sourced information it gathers. Augur has plans to make use of decentralized public ledgers to create ways for anyone to tap into the forecasting power of the user base across the world.

Using Blockchain-based Platforms for Decentralized Applications

Previously we talked about use-cases under development for using the blockchain technology. In 2015, we saw what was undoubtedly one of the biggest spikes in investment and hundreds of different startup companies have appeared on the scene, all jumping on the blockchain bandwagon. One of the biggest phenomena was when multiple blockchain platforms were developed. These are platforms that will allow third-party projects to use to core infrastructure and come up with their own products and these have been spreading fast. While some are already light years ahead in terms of usage, others are fast catching up. Some of the most notable of these platforms on which projects or integrations are being built include:

- Ethereum

- Ripple

- Eris Industries

- MaidSafe

- Stellar

- Counterparty

Other platforms that are currently paving the way for these projects to be built include:

- Blockstamp

- Hyperledger

- Epiphyte

- PeerNova

- Koinify

- Chain.com

These are the blockchain-based platforms that have been vastly utilized by others who are looking to develop brand new projects or use-cases. While some of the financial platforms, such as Stellar and Ripple, have seen a major leap in partners in the area of developing gateways for transactions, Ethereum is the company that has dominated the non-financial use case, currently running around 14 separate projects on their platform

All of this just goes to show you how the blockchain revolution is already taking off and will very soon dominate the entire world.

CHAPTER 9

5 BLOCKCHAIN TECHNOLOGY MYTHS

It is very clear that the technology behind the blockchain is going to be the most important computing invention of this generation. This is because, for the very first time in the history of the human being, we have a full digital exchange for peer-to-peer value. Blockchain is a massive global platform and is firmly based on distributed ledger. It is responsible for establishing the rules, in the format of very heavy encryption and computations, that let at least two parties carry out transactions without the need for a centralized third party agency involved to establish the trust between the parties.

Instead of being reliant on government agencies, banks or any other intermediary to create that trust, the technology that fuels the blockchain ensures that trust is provided through clever doing and collaboration on a mass scale. The trust is actually built into the blockchain system and that is why the blockchain is otherwise known as "The Trust Protocol".

If we wanted to take that a step further, the blockchain plays several other roles. It is:

- An accounts ledger

- A database

- A sentry

- A clearing house

It is, in all likelihood, going to be the second-generation internet and it has the potential to take the economic grid and rewire it to run things for the better, shaking up the old and bringing in a completely new way of working. A fresh perspective on old business systems.

Sadly, there are still a lot of myths about blockchain technology doing the rounds and these are responsible for putting a lot of influential businesses and people off of using it. Here are the top 5 of those blockchain myths, busted and explained:

1. Blockchain is good but bitcoin is bad

There are an awful lot of people, particularly in the financial sector that are very excited about the potential that blockchain technology provides. However, those same people are under the misconception that digital currencies are not feasible, they are not desirable and are in fact quite dangerous.

The blockchain for bitcoin is a permission less system, which means that anyone is able to get into it through a device that has internet access and can interact with it in the same way they do the internet. Blockchains that are permissioned, on the other hand, require that all users have specific credentials, such as an operator's license for the blockchain they want to access, and those credentials are provided by a governing body or by the members of the blockchain. These permissioned systems use the distributed ledger technology but do not have any digital currency attached to them.

At first look, the permissioned or private blockchain looks like having several advantages. For a start, members of the chain are able to make changes to the rules if they want to. They are only required to get the group they are a part of to agree to make the change, rather than having to get an entire network involved. Costs are reduced because the transactions only have to be validated by the chain members, not by that massive network. All of this can also help reduce the costs of electricity, benefitting the environments and regulators are likely to prefer them over and over the public chain, like bitcoin, because there is no need to anonymity.

But, there are some things to consider. If it is easy to change rules, it is easy to flaunt those same rules. When you limit freedoms intentionally, neutrality can be severely inhibited. If the open value innovation goes, the blockchain technology will do nothing more than stagnate and vulnerabilities will open up in it. The bitcoin blockchain, on the other hand, and any other that is tied to digital currencies, include incentives built in to encourage users to validate the transactions.

2. The financial services are the only real industry that will benefit from blockchains

Provided they are able to locate the right leadership, the FSI can alter itself using the technology behind blockchain. That technology has the potential to completely revolutionize financial services, from the humble bank account and debit card right up to the entire credit card network. If everyone is sharing the same distributed ledger, transaction settlements can happen straight away for everyone. Banks could use blockchain technology to speed up the system process and reduce the massive costs they face every day. The smartest of them will strategically use the technology, and that includes the permission less system, to get into newer markets and bring a whole bunch of new services out.

But the FSI is only a small part of the whole system. Blockchains have the potential to disrupt those that are already seen as the disrupters, like Uber. Blockchains will be at the very center of the IoT (Internet of Things) and will allow the smart device to contract with, carry out transactions and share data securely peer-to-peer.

The blockchain has the potential to completely reinvent how democracy works by ensuring that politicians have to do something they are not used to doing – be accountable to the public.

3. Blockchains are B2B (business to business) and not for the general public

So many people are convinced that blockchain technology will turn around the economy and shake up our day to day life in more ways than we could imagine. They are not just for businesses, as others believe; the blockchain will have an effect on every man, woman and child in the world today.

4. There are too many issues with blockchains to make them work

There are those who say that blockchain technology really isn't ready for the world yet. It's too difficult to use properly and the best applications are still growing, still being developed. There are others who say that there is a huge amount of energy required to get consensus across the network. They ask what would happen when millions of blockchains all connected, are processing untold numbers of transactions every day. Are there sufficient incentives in place to get people to take part and not try to overthrow the entire network? Could blockchain possibly be the biggest killer of jobs for people of all time? Instead of seeing these are bad reasons for taking on the technology, we should perhaps be looking at them as challenges of implementing the system.

5. Satoshi Nakamoto is actually Craig Wright

Craig Wright is an Australian entrepreneur who has sensationally claimed that he is the original inventor of the bitcoin, Satoshi Nakamoto. We already know that Satoshi is the only creator; there were others involved. When the first bitcoin paper was written, and the first protocol, that was what got things started. Then that person disappeared off the scene, leaving the community to keep the work going. It is that community that is responsible for most of the blockchain code and all other bitcoin-related content. In that case, everyone in the community is actually Satoshi.

This is why it doesn't really matter who the original protocol. It is a permission less system and that means there will never be an arbitrator. For the next step to be taken, the entire community has to be the governor for things to move forward. The likelihood of Craig Wright being the real Satoshi Nakamoto is very slim though

CONCLUSION

Thank you again for purchasing this book!

I hope this book was able to help you to understand what a blockchain is, the technology that underpins and the whole blockchain revolution and what it means for us.

The next step is to delve deeper into the world of blockchain technology and truly understand what the revolution is going to do for and to the world. Learn how it will revolutionize banking and financial industries, how it will have an effect on non-financial industries and how it will affect the security of future transactions.

You can see from the number of major companies and the number of startups that we have talked about in this book just how popular the technology already is. Companies like NASDAQ are not ones to jump into any old technology lightly, no without doing an awful lot of homework first and the very fact that they have gotten involved to the extent they have is a testament to the fact that blockchain technology is the future.

Thank you and good luck!

www.ingramcontent.com/pod-product-compliance
Lightning Source LLC
Chambersburg PA
CBHW071516210326
41597CB00018B/2779